The Katyn Forest Massacre: The History of th
Prisoners by the Soviets during

By Charles River Edi

A picture of Polish POWs captured by the Soviets

About Charles River Editors

Charles River Editors is a boutique digital publishing company, specializing in bringing history back to life with educational and engaging books on a wide range of topics. Keep up to date with our new and free offerings with this 5 second sign up on our weekly mailing list, and visit Our Kindle Author Page to see other recently published Kindle titles.

We make these books for you and always want to know our readers' opinions, so we encourage you to leave reviews and look forward to publishing new and exciting titles each week.

Introduction

A picture of a memorial commemorating the massacre in Poland

The Katyn Forest Massacre

"It has been suggested that the motive for this terrible step was to reassure the Germans as to the reality of Soviet anti-Polish policy. This explanation is completely unconvincing in view of the care with which the Soviet regime kept the massacre secret from the very German government it was supposed to impress…A more likely explanation is that [the massacre] should be seen as looking forward to a future in which there might again be a Poland on the Soviet Union's western border. Since he intended to keep the eastern portion of the country in any case, Stalin could be certain that any revived Poland would be unfriendly. Under those circumstances, depriving it of a large proportion of its military and technical elite would make it weaker." – Gerhard Weinberg

During the late 1930s the Soviet Union under Josef Stalin and the Third Reich under Adolf Hitler reached a secret alliance, the Molotov-Ribbentrop Pact. By the terms of this agreement, the two dictators divided up Eastern Europe between them, and for a time Stalin even sought Axis membership.

Though the alliance forged between the fascist and communist states could not survive their diametrically opposed views, they cooperated long enough to conquer Poland together in 1939. Of course, as most people now know, the invasion of Poland was merely the preface to the Nazi blitzkrieg of most of Western Europe, which would include Denmark, Belgium, and France by the summer of 1940. The resistance put up by these countries is often portrayed as weak, and the narrative is that the British stood alone in 1940 against the Nazi onslaught, defending the British Isles during the Battle of Britain and preventing a potential German invasion.

In particular, the campaign in Poland is remembered as one in which an antiquated Polish army was quickly pummeled by the world's most modern army. Polish lancers charging in a valiant yet idiotic attack against German tanks is the only image from the 1939 Nazi-Soviet invasion of Poland remaining in the popular imagination today. Originating as a piece of Nazi propaganda, paradoxically adopted by the Poles as a patriotic myth, the fictional charge obscures the actual events of September 1939. Outnumbered, outgunned, and under-equipped, the Polish army nevertheless inflicted heavy losses on the invading Wehrmacht. In fact, only the unexpected advance of Soviet forces from the east put a quick end to the struggle and saw the Polish republic partitioned again after just 20 years of independence. Nonetheless, the campaign that started World War II was a bloody sign of things to come as the conflict engulfed the globe.

While the Germans performed the lion's share of military action in defeating Poland – and reaped the choicest regions for themselves as a consequence – the Soviets showed themselves no laggards in establishing tyrannical control over the Polish zone assigned to them by treaty. NKVD death squads, mass deportations, and systematic repression began almost immediately in the Soviet-controlled part of Poland.

The Gestapo applied their own forms of brutality in the German zone of the conquered nation, but the results proved starkly different. A large-scale, well-organized Polish Resistance movement flourished in the German zone, exhibiting high morale and an activist approach that testified to the relatively amateurish nature of the Gestapo repression – random violence for intimidation rather than systematic quashing of all independence and defiance.

The NKVD, on the other hand, managed to virtually eliminate any large-scale resistance in the Russian zone. The Soviet policy proved a dark success, at least until the Wehrmacht surged crushingly across the border into the Soviet Union during the Operation Barbarossa offensive of June 1941. A key element of this policy lay in the elimination of tens of thousands of leading Poles in what became known as the Katyn Massacre or the Katyn Forest Massacre.

The massacre, a series of mass executions that murdered over 20,000 Poles, was one of the most controversial events of the war. The Soviets blamed the Nazis for the slaughter for decades, only admitting its responsibility in 1990 as the USSR was on the verge of dissolution, and even then they refused to officially find any Soviet individuals liable or responsible.

The Katyn Forest Massacre: The History of the Notorious Slaughter of Polish Prisoners by the Soviets during World War II chronicles one of the most notorious massacres of the war. Along with pictures of important people and places, you will learn about the Katyn Forest Massacre like never before.

The Katyn Forest Massacre: The History of the Notorious Slaughter of Polish Prisoners by the Soviets during World War II

About Charles River Editors

Introduction

Free Books by Charles River Editors

Discounted Books by Charles River Editors

Chapter 1: Poland Before the War

Forged from the wreck of empires following World War I, Poland represented both a practical and a symbolic stumbling block to the ambitions of both Nazi and Soviet leaders by the late 1930s. Prussia, Austria, and Russia had extinguished Polish sovereignty on October 24th, 1795 with the "Third Partition," absorbing the Polish Commonwealth into their respective empires, and a secret treaty clause pledged all three powers to work to permanently "abolish" the existence of Poland. With that, the imperial partners drove many leading Poles into exile, but nevertheless, Polish patriotism survived, flourishing underground and emerging periodically. The Polish aided Napoleon Bonaparte with superb lancer cavalry, relishing the chance to strike back at the loathed Russians, Prussians, and Austrians, but while the Poles also hoped for restoration of their Republic, this did not occur until over 100 years after the Napoleonic Era.

The fall of the German and Russian empires in 1917 and 1918 presented Poland with its opportunity. Led by Jozef Piłsudski, the Poles founded a democratic nation in 1918 with the blessing of the Western Allies. However, the emergent, blood-soaked dictatorship of the Soviet Union took a far different view of Poland's resurrection: "[I]n spring 1920, Lenin and Trotsky thought that they would bring their own revolution to Poland, using the bayonet to inspire workers to fulfill their historical role. After Poland's fall, German comrades, assisted by the new Red Army, would bring to bear Germany's vast resources to save the Russian revolution. But the Soviet forces on their way to Berlin were halted by the Polish Army at Warsaw in August 1920." (Snyder, 2010, 24).

Piłsudski

Already a violent, unscrupulous aggressor, the Soviet Union aimed to scoop up Poland on the way to its actual prize: Germany and the rest of Europe. Initially, the Soviets enjoyed military success, battering their way deep into Polish territory, and the Soviets' triumphalist language left scant doubt as to their intentions. Besides openly crowing that Berlin, Paris, and London headed their objective list, the communists exulted in the prostration of Poland. On July 2, 1920, General Mikhail N. Tukhachevsky told his men, "Over the corpse of White Poland lies the road to worldwide conflagration. March on Vilno, Minsk, Warsaw!"

Tukhachevsky

The tentatively pro-Soviet Prime Minister of Britain, David Lloyd George, scuppered plans to aid the Poles with arms shipments against the onrushing Bolsheviks, but Pilsudski and his colleague Wladyslaw Sikorsky refused to admit defeat. Armed with deciphered Soviet radio communications, the Polish commanders lured Tukhachevsky into an overextended position near Warsaw in August. From August 14-18, 1920, the Polish armies executed a massive encircling movement, defeating the Russians in the span of just five days. The Battle of Komarow provided the action's centerpiece; in history's last true cavalry battle, eight Soviets died for every Pole killed in action as Sikorsky's Uhlans (lancers) smashed Soviet Marshal Semyon Budyonny's dreaded 1st Cavalry Army to pieces.

Sikorsky

The war continued for some time, until finally the Russians signed a treaty in March 1921 that ended the hostilities and recognized the existence of Poland as a separate nation. That said, Poland's victory represented more of a respite than a permanent triumph; the nation, positioned between two strengthening dictatorships just a decade later in the 1930s, represented a staging area for Germany's eastward "Lebensraum" plans and the Soviets' westward "Red Europe" dreams: "Poland changed the balance of power in eastern Europe. It was not large enough to be a great power, but it was large enough to be a problem for any great power with plans of expansion. It separated Russia from Germany, for the first time in more than a century. Poland's very existence created a buffer to both Russian and German power, and was much resented in Moscow and Berlin." (Snyder, 2010, 22).

The Austrians and Czechoslovakians put up little to no resistance to Hitler's advance, but Poland offered a more serious challenge. Though in a very difficult situation, the Poles refused to yield their sovereignty without a vigorous fight. Starting in 1937, the Poles commenced a massive rearmament program, spearheaded by the construction of new factories at Starachowice, Rzeszow, and other locations. Production centered on 37mm anti-tank guns and 40mm anti-aircraft guns, but the Poles also fabricated other weapons systems in a hasty bid for deterrence and war preparation.

Money problems and a heavy reliance on imported raw materials hampered Poland's efforts at building an army. Shortages forced military contractors to produce the most urgent items first. Thus, the factories rolled out considerable numbers of 37mm anti-tank guns, but they could not spare the industrial capacity to make trucks or halftracks to tow them into action. Horses therefore towed most of Poland's anti-tank guns. Horses are slower than trucks, and they understandably tend to panic at the sound of loud explosions. The artillery required additional horses to carry ammunition and spare parts, all of which was more efficiently transported in towing trucks by the German army.

Some factors worked in Poland's favor, however. Polish experts, working from a civilian Enigma machine obtained earlier, contrived to keep abreast of German coding procedures throughout the 1930s. Despite multiple upgrades to the cryptographic technology by the Nazis, the Poles soon deciphered each fresh advance and thus obtained vast quantities of high quality intelligence on German plans and movements. "The Germans had a blind faith in their technical invincibility and consequently, at times, made careless mistakes [...] In January 1938 the Poles found that they could read 75 per cent of the Wehrmacht's cable traffic. By the summer the Poles had an impressive new code centre in the Kabackie Woods near Warsaw. A French officer, Captain Bertrand, remembered: '[...] this was the brain centre of the organization where work went on day and night in silence.'" (Williamson, 2009, 31).

The Polish military built up a stock of vehicles as well, but obviously the Poles could not match the tremendous mechanization program of the Third Reich. Aircraft, tanks, and similar hardware rolled off Polish production lines in modest numbers, and among the vehicles the Poles built were 575 TKS "tankettes." These strange little armored fighting vehicles featured a square plan, continuous caterpillar tracks, a weight of 2.6 tons, and a crew of two. Somewhat amusing in appearance, these miniature tanks mostly carried 7.62mm machine guns and served mostly as scout vehicles and mobile machine gun nests for infantry support. The Poles improved the guns on a minority of these TKS vehicles with 20mm cannons, which proved surprisingly lethal against 6-ton Panzer I and 8.8-ton Panzer II tanks. Described vividly as "cockroaches against panzers" by Polish historians, these tankettes even offered an opportunity for an "ace" to emerge in Roman Orlik, whose "cockroach" claimed a total of 13 Panzers during the 1939 invasion.

A TKS

Orlik

Poland's preparations, though energetic, failed to keep pace with the industrial might of Nazi Germany or even the backward but immense Soviet Union. Recognizing their relative weakness, the Poles sought a diplomatic solution, bolstering their strength with that of allies.

German preparations for the seizure of Polish territory or outright annexation of Poland proceeded rapidly throughout 1938 and into 1939. The Third Reich's rearmament program was underway in any case, providing cover for a military buildup near the Polish border.

Diplomatically, the German state pursued several goals simultaneously. Hitler, through intermediaries such as the slippery Joachim von Ribbentrop, sought to obfuscate his actual intent by periodically floating the idea of an anti-Soviet alliance with the Poles when talks occurred between representatives of the two nations. At the same time, von Ribbentrop regularly brought up the subject of handing over the Baltic city of Danzig and the nearby territories to Nazi control, which the alarmed Poles managed to evade while holding out hope they might comply in the near future.

Joachim von Ribbentrop

This diplomatic dance served as a mask for Hitler's purposes even as it gave the Poles a few more precious months to prepare. All the while, uncertainty about the Nazi dictator's attitude towards Poland kept the French and British from action; in fact, they sent less aid to Poland than they were inclined to for fear of disturbing a highly delicate situation. Of course, since Hitler commanded much greater industrial power than Poland, these delays ultimately aided German preparations more than those of Poland. For example, the Luftwaffe possessed 4,093 serviceable fighters, bombers, and dive-bombers on the eve of the Polish invasion, while the Poles mustered just 397. "Bomber strength was only about 20 per cent of the projected numbers and observation planes only about two-thirds of the intended figure. Although the number of fighter planes was theoretically up to strength, many were obsolescent. In general, the Polish Air Force was not capable of an offensive role." (Williamson, 2009, 25).

The Poles, understandably, remained highly suspicious of their brutal, relentless neighbors to the east, the Soviet Russians. If anything, Bolshevism represented a more alien and menacing philosophy to Polish culture than Nazism, or at least it seemed that way in 1939. The Poles maintained a non-aggression treaty with the USSR, but they were also keenly aware of its fragility.

Playing it safe, the Polish high command drew up defensive plans for an attack by either the Germans or the Soviets, but in a curious oversight, none of Poland's military planners thought to come up with a plan for a two-front war in case both of the nation's neighbors attacked simultaneously.

As it turned out, that oversight would prove disastrous. When Chamberlain visited Hitler in September 1938, Stalin became convinced that England was planning a secret pact with Germany against the Soviet Union, so he decided to try to beat them to the punch; Stalin contacted Hitler and proposed that they form an alliance, going as far as to fire his Commissar of Foreign Affairs, Maxim Litinov, a Jew who was an unacceptable ambassador to Hitler's government. Thus, throughout much of the first half of 1939, the Nazis (represented by their Moscow ambassador Friedrich Werner von der Schulenburg) and the Soviets (fronted by Stalin's diplomatic crony Vyacheslav Molotov, after whom partisans ironically named Molotov cocktails) engaged in wary, nebulous negotiations. Both powers indicated the need for political and economic cooperation, but they gave each other no concrete details; the two dictatorships clearly experienced profound distrust and were unwilling to even indicate to one another what they were willing to negotiate about.

Friedrich Werner von der Schulenburg

Molotov

With plans afoot for the invasion of Poland, Hitler pushed hard to acquire a treaty with Stalin. Molotov and Stalin initially delayed, but they finally agreed to meet Ribbentrop on August 23rd, 1939 to sign a mutual non-aggression and trade treaty which contained a secret clause regarding the annexation of Poland.

The secret clause seems, from Soviet communications, to have originated with the Soviets, and probably from a personal command of Josef Stalin delivered verbally to Molotov. It was not revealed to the world until the western Allies defeated the Nazis in 1945 and captured the treaty document, but with a flourish of their pens, Ribbentrop and Molotov abolished Poland yet again. Negotiations about earlier parts of the treaty proved lengthy and tedious, but both sides agreed to the secret clause within a few hours on the same day Ribbentrop flew into Moscow.

Though the negotiations themselves went smoothly, Stalin still put his foot down regarding some of Ribbentrop's flights of diplomatic fancy, indicating that the wounds between the two dictatorships were very far from healed under the veneer of unanimity. "[A] high-falutin preamble which Ribbentrop wanted to insert stressing the formation of friendly Soviet-German relations was thrown out at the insistence of Stalin. The Soviet dictator complained that 'the Soviet government could not suddenly present to the public assurances of friendship after they had been covered with pails of manure by the Nazi government for six years.'" (Shirer, 2011, 539).

The treaty ensuring the demise of Poland bore the name Molotov-Ribbentrop Pact, but Molotov wisely deferred to his murderous master, Stalin, on every point during the process of hammering out the exact terms by which an entire nation was doomed. The negotiations concluded with a fulsome display of false camaraderie between Ribbentrop, Stalin, and Molotov: "Stalin spontaneously proposed a toast to the Fuehrer: 'I know how much the German nation loves its Fuehrer. I should therefore like to drink to his health.' Molotov drank to the health of the Reich Foreign Minister ... Molotov and Stalin drank repeatedly to the Nonaggression Pact, the new era of German–Russian relations, and to the German nation. The Reich Foreign Minister in turn proposed a toast to Stalin." (Shirer, 2011, 532).

Molotov signing the pact

A picture of Stalin shaking hands with Ribbentrop

After a convivial evening with the man who had ordered the shooting deaths of 600,000 or more Soviet citizens on the flimsiest pretexts and the starvation of some three million Ukrainians, Ribbentrop flew back to Berlin in a buoyant mood. Nazi Germany found itself free to strike at Poland, though Hitler would end up delaying the attack until September 1st.

The Molotov-Ribbentrop Pact laid out the respective spheres of influence each imperial power claimed within Poland, using rivers as boundaries. The signatories attached their signatures so quickly that some of the geographic descriptions later proved erroneous. The Russians and Germans agreed on amendments to the secret protocol in order to make the division of Poland match up to actual topography. Just 18 years after pushing the Red Army out of their territory, the Poles were about to find a new horde rolling across their borders, bent on slaughter and conquest.

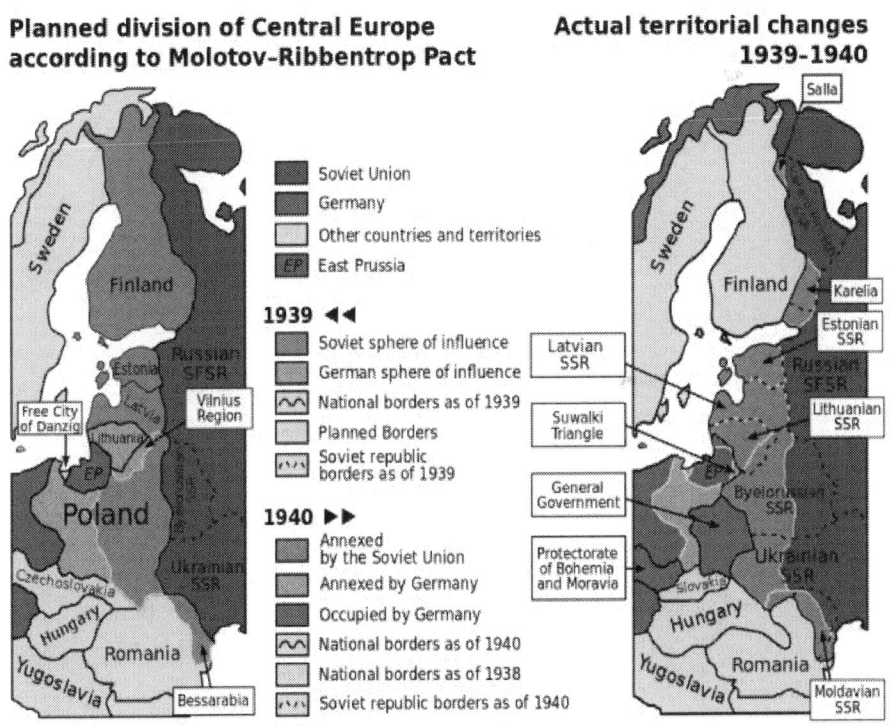

Peter Hanula's map of the plan to divide Poland

Even with the treaty signed and toasts drunk to its success, Molotov continued to play a double game. He dangled the possibility of fresh negotiations in front of the Poles even after the invasion started, decisively severing ties only when it became clear the Germans would succeed in conquering Poland. "Reluctance to give in to German pressure, to make the collaboration of the two powers official, continued after Germany attacked Poland and Britain and France declared war. As late as 5 September, Molotov offered aid to W. Grzybowski, the Polish ambassador. With the rapid collapse of Polish resistance, however, he refused to see Grzybowski for two days, then on 8 September withdrew the offer." (Watson, 2005, 171).

Meanwhile, the British and French envoys arriving in Moscow to negotiate with Stalin shortly thereafter found themselves peremptorily rebuffed with the news that the Soviet Union was no longer interested in major treaties with them. This news prompted an explosion of alarm and outrage in the government offices of London and Paris. Clearly, something insidious had taken place, and the Allies began to fear an imminent outbreak of war.

Chapter 2: The Invasion of Poland

Huge numbers of German soldiers moved up to the Polish border as the invasion date approached. Hitler's Wehrmacht already included separate Panzer divisions whose goal was not infantry support but deep, rapid penetration of enemy territory for sweeping encircling movements. This style of warfare, known as Blitzkrieg or lightning war, was nothing new, but the Germans were the first to use it on a large scale with mechanized forces. General George S. Patton would use similar tactics to badly maul Nazi armies in western Europe just a few years later.

Heading into September 1939, the Poles had a very scant conception of the type of adversary poised to crush their nation. For all their glaring faults, the empires partitioning Poland in the 18th century had not viewed the Polish people as vermin to be massacred, but Hitler, on the other hand, made his views clear in a speech to his inner circle of generals one day prior to the signing of the Molotov-Ribbentrop Pact's in Moscow: "Our strength lies in our speed and our brutality. Genghis Khan hunted millions of women and children to their deaths, consciously and with a joyous heart. [...] I have put my Death's Head formations at the ready with the command to send man, woman and child of Polish descent and language to their deaths, pitilessly and remorselessly. Poland will be depopulated and settled with Germans." (Evans, 2009, 27).

As Hitler's words suggest, the Wehrmacht was not prepared or terribly interested in distinguishing between military and civilian targets. During the campaign, the Luftwaffe would strafe columns of civilian refugees, clearly identified as such, operating as though the civilians were advancing military formations. German tanks would fire into hospitals marked with the Red Cross emblem, and German units would round up large numbers of men, women and children and shoot them out of hand or lock them in churches or barns and set them on fire.

Joseph Goebbels' propaganda bears a considerable measure of blame for these hate-fueled actions. The Poles did indeed kill slightly more than 2,000 ethnic Germans during the first days of the invasion, a definite war crime (albeit a relatively limited one compared to the staggering atrocities of the Nazis or Soviets) but Goebbels, Hitler's propaganda minister, inflated the number killed to over 600,000, generating vast hostility towards the Poles among ordinary German soldiers.

Goebbels

Hitler originally intended his attack on Poland to occur on August 26th, 1939. The Fuhrer clearly wanted a tight timetable offering the Poles as little opportunity as possible to prepare, respond, or send out a call for help. Ribbentrop arrived in Moscow and signed the Molotov-Ribbentrop Pact on August 23rd, then flew back to Germany on August 24th. Hitler's plan to cross the border on the 26th, just two days later, would give the German forces deployed there just enough time to muster and move out.

However, British actions caused Hitler a brief hesitation and ultimately shifted the invasion back to September 1st, 1939, the date when the border crossing actually commenced. These rapid deployments were possible because the Germans began preparing as early as March 1939, when Hitler first reached the decision to invade Poland. In the meantime, forces gathered along Poland's southern border in freshly-conquered Czechoslovakia, on the west inside Germany itself, and on the north in the detached German possession of East Prussia.

The British Parliament passed the Emergency Powers Defense Bill on August 24th, 1939, which declared England's continued intention to support Poland's independent existence. Though the Third Reich and the USSR kept the clauses of the Molotov-Ribbentrop Pact related to the partition of Poland secret, the British shrewdly guessed that something of the kind might have been agreed on. The Emergency Powers Defense Bill, and the letter Neville Chamberlain sent to Hitler regarding it, referenced the Molotov-Ribbentrop Pact, stating that its existence made no difference to England's resolve to help the Poles in case of aggression.

As a result, Hitler pushed back the invasion date – "Case White" – to September 1st while he attempted to deal with the British. Simultaneously, he contacted Benito Mussolini, the fascist Italian "Duce," and hinted broadly that he hoped for Italian military support. Given the pitiful quality of Mussolini's armies, and the outstanding strength and modernity of the Wehrmacht, this appeal looks faintly absurd. He also made a strange offer to the British ambassador, Nevile Henderson: "He desired to make a move toward England which should be as decisive as the move towards Russia … The Fuehrer is ready to conclude agreements with England which would not only guarantee the existence of the British Empire in all circumstances so far as Germany is concerned, but would also if necessary assure the British Empire of German assistance regardless of where such assistance should be necessary." (Shirer, 2011, 543).

Henderson

The British ignored Hitler's strange offer and signed a fresh treaty of mutual support with Poland. Around the same time, Mussolini politely rebuffed the Fuhrer's latest overtures, claiming his involvement in the Balkans and North Africa was too deep to permit aiding the Germans. Thus, Hitler, unsure of what to do, called off the attack a few hours before its scheduled beginning.

Immediately before the September 1st attack, the Germans carried out a "false flag" operation to provide a pretext for their Polish invasion. This grotesque plan involved bringing concentration camp prisoners to the border, dressing them in uniforms, and then murdering them at German posts near the border to represent "casualties" inflicted during fictitious Polish raids across the border into Germany. The Germans executed this plan, known as "Operation Himmler" (named after SS head Heinrich Himmler), with their usual efficiency, though nobody honestly fell for the false flag. "Heinrich Mueller, the head of the Gestapo, was put in charge of these operations. It was part of the plan that a number of prisoners from concentration camps should be dressed in Polish uniforms, given fatal injections by a doctor and at the right moment shot [...]. These victims were to be brought in under the code-words 'canned goods'. Their bodies were to be photographed for publication." (Manvell, 2007, 77).

Himmler

Mueller

These Polish "attacks" offered Hitler his excuse for a war that he had planned as far back as six months ago, and the atrocity was apparently a last minute effort to convince the British not to declare war. In this, it naturally failed, but Hitler placed no value on his prisoners' lives and seemed, at times, as though he wished to explore the furthest possible reaches of amoral disregard for human life, rights, or dignity.

Although the campaign in Poland is typically overlooked, especially in comparison to some of the incredibly large and violent campaigns in subsequent years, it was instrumental in providing the Nazi forces with experience they would use across Europe and in Russia. After all, it was in Poland that the Wehrmacht saw action for the first time, conducting what was not only an invasion but also a trial run of its new equipment and tactics. The Polish invasion proved invaluable in providing the German high command with a low-risk, high-value live fire exercise for their newly minted war machine, while the actual combat experience highlighted the remaining flaws in the system. During the campaign, the Germans honed tactics and weapon systems for the massive struggle with the Soviets, British, and United States that loomed on the horizon.

For their part, the Poles predicated their strategy on fighting a delaying action in the west, accompanied by a slow withdrawal eastward. The Poles still believed the Soviets would not attack them; in fact, a few Polish leaders, more sanguine than the rest, thought the Russians might send aid to them to help expel the Germans. They also trusted their new alliance with the British and French to provide speedy relief. Both of these Polish hopes proved hollow.

Technology and military doctrine both favored the Germans in the context of the era as well. The Germans considered communication key to good battlefield coordination and control, so radios were very commonplace. The Third Reich built large numbers of its tanks with individual radios, in contrast to the radio-free tanks of Poland. The Wehrmacht also made extensive use of radios in infantry units, and commanders, artillerymen, and spotters used radio communications to launch precise, timely fire missions to soften the way for their own attacks or halt those of the enemy.

In terms of doctrine, the Germans were years in advance of the Poles. Polish tanks were spread thin, assigned to supporting infantry units. The Germans clustered their armor assets into Panzer divisions which operated independently, striking rapidly and deeply into enemy territory and applying a concentration of force and firepower the Poles simply could not emulate with their diffuse armor deployments.

The Poles' main advantages included home ground knowledge, courage, and decent quality small arms, including rifles copied from German models and machine guns based on American designs. Led by an ossified high command that fled almost as soon as the war opened, hampered by lack of radios, equipment, vehicles, and a modern air force, the Poles' only hope was to hold out long enough for some other power to come to their aid. Despite the loud assurances of the British and French, it wouldn't happen.

Over the course of the next six days, the situation worsened for the Poles and improved for the Germans. The Wehrmacht, well-equipped and highly motivated but inexperienced, continued to suffer considerable losses in both men and tanks, but the German armies remained a cohesive and effective fighting force.

On the other hand, the combat and deeply penetrating pincer movements rapidly degraded the ability of the Poles to keep resisting. The Polish air force, though gallant, died in flames where they crashed in the Polish countryside after being shot down by their German counterparts. Indeed, the Luftwaffe was the most elite arm of the Germany military at the start of the war, due in large part to the fact "they had the benefit of modern combat experience fed back from their *Legion Condor* contributions to the victory of General Franco's forces in Spain. In particular, many of the theories of army cooperation and close air support were put to the practical test and invaluable lessons absorbed." (Smith, 1998, 5). The Polish soldiers soon learned that venturing out onto roads in daylight was certain death, as any column of Polish infantry, cavalry, or vehicles was soon spotted by the Germans. Using their radios, the Wehrmacht called in the location to the Luftwaffe, whose terrible dive-bombers soon appeared to spread slaughter among the men trapped in the flat, open Polish countryside under the light of day.

Nevertheless, the need to retreat remained the driving imperative behind Polish strategy. The overall "grand strategy" of Poland was to fight a delaying action while retreating to fortified positions in the east. There, the Poles would dig in and wait for the French and British to come to their rescue by invading Germany, forcing Hitler to pull back his armies in order to protect his homeland, people, and logistical base. Moreover, the rapid encircling movements also made retreat the sole option for remaining free and alive for a few days longer. Once the double trap of the two grand Wehrmacht sweeps crashed shut, the Polish armies would be trapped in large pockets across the countryside, subject to either mass surrender or hopeless defeat in detail.

That said, actually carrying out the retreat wore down the ability of the Polish army to resist. During the daylight hours, the Poles found movement impossible under the hawk-like vigilance of the Luftwaffe. Remaining in one place, however, meant they were attacked by the Germans, forcing them to fight for much of the day. The Poles found it was possible to engage in movement free from Stuka attacks at night, but this forced the men to remain awake almost 24 hours a day. After a few days of this, the Poles were so exhausted that they began to fight more poorly, move more slowly, and suffer from lower morale and a sense of fatigue-drenched hopelessness.

With so many disadvantages weighing against them, the Poles could not maintain their defense for more than a few days, regardless of their courage and occasional local successes. Within four to five days, Polish command at all levels lost communications contact with both headquarters and with other Polish formations elsewhere in the country. Given this lack of strategic coordination, the Poles found themselves fighting blind against a highly coordinated foe whose command of the skies gave them almost total information regarding troop movements and strategic developments. "The dam burst: German mechanised columns plunged deep into Polish lines, and on 7 September the tanks of the 4th Panzer Division began appearing outside the suburbs of Warsaw. They began immediately to make attempts to break into the city itself, but showed little judgement, and on 9 September alone the Poles claimed 57 tanks from the 4th Panzer Division in intense street fighting. The second week of the war went just as badly." (Zaloga, 1982, 10).

Nazi soldiers posing with captured civilians

The ruins of the Polish city of Wieluń

The Battle of the Bzura represented the last hurrah for the defending Polish forces. From that point on, they slid rapidly towards defeat, thanks to the combination of factors which had led to their plight during the first two weeks of the invasion. Another event sealed the doom of Poland even more assuredly; the Soviet Army, 446,000 men strong, rolled across the border into Poland on September 17 across a front 850 miles wide.

Approximately 100,000 reservists held the eastern frontier against this surprise attack, but these men were in the process of training and had only light weapons at their disposal. Polish high command sent the order to them to negotiate with the Soviets and seek safe passage to Romania. The chief generals of Poland realized that with this new force advancing from the east, their position was untenable. Ordering the reservists to fight would only result in needless butchery, with the outcome precisely the same in any case. The Soviets, however, had not come to talk. Like the Germans, they moved with a grim purpose and viewed the Poles as little more than an obstacle to their overall plans, rather than as human beings. When the reservists attempted to negotiate passage to Romania or Hungary, the Soviet soldiers simply attacked them, forcing them to fight.

The reservists, half-trained and lightly armed, suffered tremendous losses against the Soviet armies. The Russians' tactics were simple and their coordination poor, thanks to Stalin's butchery of his own officer corps during the recent "Great Purge." However, a sort of Darwinian selection occurred by which semi-capable officers came to the fore and received promotions due to the fact that they were tactically acute enough to survive combat. The famous Georgi Zhukov, who would later lead the Soviet armies against Germany, was one of these emergent leaders.

Zhukov

By September 20, Poland's armies were effectively defeated in both the west and the east. Warsaw held out heroically for some time, but by October 6, the nation of Poland had all but ceased to exist. It now only remained for the victorious Nazis and Soviets to divide up the spoils and decide what was to be done with the unfortunate population. Poland, which had emerged from centuries of servitude in the wake of World War I, had found itself subjected to foreign conquerors again in 1939. Indeed, the men who now ruled its fate were far crueler than any who had come over its borders since the days of the Mongol hordes.

A picture of German and Soviet soldiers shaking hands in Poland

In the west, Britain and France had declared war on Germany, but they ultimately did nothing to aid their Polish allies. Their promises to hasten to the Poles' assistance in the event of foreign attack proved to be worth no more than the breath expended speaking them and the paper they were written on. The French advanced a few miles into Germany, seizing some unoccupied forest, but French soldiers refused to move outside the range of the artillery mounted in the Maginot Line, even though nearly every German soldier was redeployed hundreds of miles to the east.

The French command noted that Hitler's new method of warfare was nearly "Napoleonic" in its nature and further added, "The frontline does not exist any more and is replaced by a three-dimensional space extending on all the territory occupied by the fighting armies. Consequently the linear disposition of the troops along the frontier seems to appear totally wrong [. . .] The vital forces of the enemy have to be gradually destroyed. Their blows have to be answered by blows [. . .] The fight should be carried by independent groups of great units." (Williamson, 2009, 195).

However, despite clearly realizing (and even enunciating) this, the French acted in precisely the opposite manner by putting their full faith in a linear disposition of troops along the frontier and in fixed fortifications. A few days after venturing unwillingly over the border into Germany, the "Gallic cockerel" scuttled back ignominiously to the relative safety of the French border defenses, where the French would await their own turn on the chopping block of Hitler's insatiable aggression. With that feeble gesture, the attempts of the British and French to come to the aid of Poles abruptly ended.

In the face of defeat, the Polish government and around 150,000 of its soldiers fled abroad, ostensibly to continue the fight another day. Though many soldiers who decamped did indeed make good on this promise by fighting bravely alongside the British during the D-Day landings and the liberating drive through Europe in 1944 and 1945, the actions of the Polish government were much less defensible. The lack of modern radio communications, coupled with poor planning, had rendered the Polish command structure superfluous just a few days into the campaign. "The reality was that by the end of the first week of fighting the Polish High Command had lost control and contact with most units. Plans for counter-offensive actions tended to be overtaken by German successes. The Commander-in-Chief Marshal Rydz-Smigly was an unimaginative leader, timorous and unwilling to take risks. Several opportunities had been lost by him for counter-offensive action, most notably one for the Army Poznan to strike south in defence of Warsaw." (Prazmowska, 1995, 3).

Chapter 3: Arrest and Deportation of the Poles

Once Hitler and Stalin conquered Poland, further negotiations took place to refine their shared boundaries. Joachim von Ribbentrop, the slippery, gloating Axis negotiator, once again flew east to meet with Molotov and Stalin. "The collapse of Poland prefaced Ribbentrop's second visit to Moscow, which marked the high point of Nazi–Soviet friendship. On 20 September, after an alarm over where the Germans would draw the demarcation line between the zones of influence of the two powers, Molotov told Schulenburg that the USSR believed that 'the time was ripe' for the two powers to establish a permanent new structure for the Polish area." (Watson, 2005. 173).

While the Nazis would never be mistaken for humane, Hitler's Wehrmacht treated the Polish people with astonishing brutality considering their close genetic and even cultural ties to German border regions. Poland's high Jewish population explains some of this mayhem, since approximately 10% of the people living in Poland at the time belonged to this religion, at least nominally. However, the Nazis viewed the blond, blue-eyed, Christian Poles as being just as subhuman as the Jews they lived alongside. 65,000 Polish civilians were shot, burned, or otherwise massacred before the end of 1939, with more to follow. The new German government lowered Polish wages to near-starvation levels, while confiscation, plundering, and rape grew endemic.

The Poles who found themselves in the areas under Soviet control would fare little better. Though communism nominally preached the brotherhood of humankind and the Soviets did not embrace the concept of racial cleansing, they still viewed the Poles as little more than revolting capitalist chattel in need of brutal reeducation. Indeed, the Soviets would approach this matter with their typical lack of restraint

When the Soviets took over the eastern area of Poland in September 1939, they immediately began a process of wholesale, systematic plundering of the same type exhibited in 1945 throughout their new Eastern European empire. Soviet teams disassembled entire Polish factories for shipment to the USSR, but the looting did not stop there, however. The Russians harvested the choicest timber in the eastern Polish forests, stripped the fields of crops – including truckloads of cabbages – and took vast consignments of furniture, tools, and household utensils from the homes of ordinary Poles. Soviet teams even pried up floorboards and loaded them in stacks on railway cars for shipment to Russia. The Russians carried out this plundering swiftly, efficiently, and with a minimum of wastage.

Molotov, Stalin's right-hand man and toady, issued a statement declaring that the Soviets undertook the invasion in order "to take all measures to extricate the Polish People from the unfortunate war into which they were dragged by their unwise leaders, and to enable them to lead a peaceful life." (FitzGibbon, 1971, 22). At the same time, the Soviets took a number of Polish officers and other leading citizens into custody, sending them to POW camps in Russia.

Ultimately, the main push to imprison the potential leaders of Polish resistance came on the night of December 9, 1939. During the previous months, the NKVD gathered intelligence regarding the location of concealed Polish officers, and by early December, they had the information necessary to arrest thousands, then tens of thousands. On that bitterly cold night in the second week of December, trucks driven by armed NKVD soldiers fanned out through the streets of Polish cities. At houses marked in the preceding days by NKVD agents as the hideouts of Polish officers or other "enemies of the state" (such as policemen, intellectuals, and certain teachers), the trucks stopped. A squad of around a dozen NKVD soldiers armed with rifles poured out, beat on the door, and forced their way in if the occupants did not open it.

This series of arrests, carried out around 1:00-2:00 a.m. in the early morning hours of December 10 in order to catch its targets unprepared, yielded huge numbers of prisoners. The Soviets placed these men into overcrowded prisons prior to their transfer to POW camps in Russia itself, and one of them, Wladyslaw Anders, who survived to lead a free Polish corps in the British Army later in the war, described the conditions in these jails: "Though the winter was a severe one, the temperature being 30° C below freezing-point [-21° F], I was not given my uniform but was put into a thin drill overall. A warden brought in a bucket of water, which immediately froze, and another bucket for excrement […] Occasionally, a piece of bread was thrown in to me and I was given a plate of a horrid liquid pompously called soup." (Anders, 1949, 23).

In all, the Soviets collected approximately 14,500 men, mostly Polish Army officers or rank-and-file, or policemen. Some professors, writers, and judges also found their way into the

NKVD's hands. Inquiries about the location of these prisoners began almost immediately, and from several sources. The Polish government in exile in England, led by Wladyslaw Sikorski, wanted to know the fate of the prisoners, as did their families and the Polish communist organizations that the Soviets already began assembling. The Soviets responded by either stating that all the prisoners had already been set at liberty, or by saying that they had no information about what had happened to them. Tens of thousands of other men – ordinary soldiers of Belarusian and Ukrainian origin – in fact received release by the Soviets, who had no political interest in them and viewed them as an oppressed underclass likely to adopt Bolshevism.

The Soviets sent the 14,500 men to three camps, Kozelsk, Starobilsk, and Ostashkov. 7,300 more prisoners found themselves immured in NKVD prisons in Ukraine, at such locations as Kiev and other cities. All three camps used former monasteries for their main facilities, though in some cases the Soviets also incorporated nearby, more recent buildings into the complexes, and the NKVD segregated the prisoners by profession to some degree between the three camps.

Lavrenty Beria placed a personal friend, First Deputy Commissar of State Security Vsevolod Merkulov, in charge of the camps. The Soviets used intensive interviews and infiltration by agents to learn as much as possible about the individual prisoners. Some historians speculate the purpose of this information gathering centered mainly on identifying the relatives of the men so they could be rounded up and deported to Kazakhstan, effectively silencing their questions about the fate of the prisoners.

Merkulov

During the interrogation process, the NKVD selected a small handful of men for recruitment into the communist Polish army then under formation in the Soviet Union. Though no exact record of the identification procedure is known at present, the NKVD clearly had their techniques of filtering out the minority of soldiers and police most likely to accept Bolshevik doctrine and later assist in the creation of a communist Poland. Out of the 3,920 officers, reservists, and cadets at Starobilsk, the Soviets chose 79 men to live (2%). 245 soldiers from Kozelsk found their way into Soviet service, out of a total of around 4,500 men initially earmarked for execution (5.4%). From Ostashkov's large prisoner population of 6,500 policemen, frontier guards, judges, teachers, writers, and military police, the NKVD only chose 124 men as worthy of survival (1.9%).

Conditions at the camps showed the same ghastliness as the NKVD prison that Wladyslaw Anders endured. From the beginning, shortages of everything prevailed, including bunk beds, forcing many of the men to take turns sleeping on the floor. Food consisted of thin lentil soup, or thin fish soup made with small pieces of rotten fish, and a piece of black bread, usually sopping wet. Rather naively for a Soviet officer, Captain Berezkov, commandant of Starobilsk camp, asked his superiors for a copy of the "Doctors'" Geneva Conventions. He wished to use the document to help him cope with the unfamiliar demands of running a prisoner-of-war camp. He received a curt response which effectively stated the Geneva Conventions did not apply to the prisoners: "The Doctors' Geneva Convention is not the document by which you shall be guided in your practical work. In your work you are to follow the instructions of the Directorate of the NKVD for Prisoners of War." (Ellis, 2015, 113).

Starobilsk

The Soviets forced the men to work to improve their own camps, a typical NKVD measure which saved the state money. Despite living on starvation rations, the Poles found themselves obliged to haul heavy timbers to strengthen the dilapidated buildings, and to build new, expanded bunk beds to accommodate the overcrowded prisoner population. The Poles received a meager wage for their efforts, and, after a few weeks, the Soviets set up commissary shops at the camps. While these offered useful items and even supplemental food for sale, supply never kept pace with demand. Often, the camp guards got first choice of each consignment as it arrived, and in any case all items typically sold out almost immediately despite the low amount of money possessed by individual Poles.

To keep the men from escaping, besides their displacement deep into Russian territory, the Soviets built enclosures around the former monasteries. Four wooden towers stood around the camp, forming the points of an outer quadrangle. These towers mounted searchlights and machine guns. Thick barbed wire entanglements filled the spaces between the towers, interspersed with raised sentry boxes occupied by heavily armed NKVD troops.

The Soviets overlooked religious observances initially, enabling the Poles – most of them highly religious at the time – to continue openly practicing the rituals of their faith. The arrest of various religious figures such as priests and rabbis made these observances easier. One man, who survived to tell his story due to his selection for recruitment into Polish communist forces, later asserted, "Prisoners of the Mosaic [Jewish], Protestant, and Orthodox faiths participated en masse in Catholic services [...] and joined in the fraternal singing of religious hymns." (Cienciala, 2007, 33).

The Soviets soon noticed these events, however. As militant atheists, at least nominally in the case of individuals, the NKVD men quickly suppressed the religious ceremonies. Soon afterward, the Russians removed all 45 of the religious officiants, Protestant, Catholic, and Jewish, from the camps. Only three returned to Poland alive, and an American officer brought later to view the Katyn mass graves saw at least one corpse dressed in the cassock of a Roman Catholic priest.

Thus, the Poles continued to carry out their religious practices in secret. They also played cards among themselves, though the puritanical Soviets, opposed to all forms of enjoyment, forbade this "bourgeois" activity. Some of the Polish officers urged their fellow inmates to continue speaking Polish and to refuse to talk in Russian as an act of defiance against their captors. The prisoners observed several minutes of silence every night at 9:00 p.m. to allow prayer or personal reflection, as one anonymous survivor recounted: "A silence fell as at the Consecration of the Host during Mass. [...] I remember one occasion when an NKVD captain entered our church building during the minutes of silence. He was taken aback, and asked one of the prisoners for an explanation, and the echoes of his voice [...] seemed to fill every corner of the building, [...] increasing the weird effect. Then, after five minutes, the human beehive returned to normal life, everyone moving and shouting again." (FitzGibbon, 1971, 39).

Declaring themselves Allied combatants, the Poles lobbied the Soviets unceasingly to release them to the British or French. The Soviets, of course, completely ignored these demands. Instead, they continued their interrogations, using teams led by NKVD officer Vasily Zarubin, known to the Poles as "Kombrig" or "The Kombrig." Zarubin's teams interviewed each prisoner a minimum of four or five times, with Zarubin handling the questioning of men the Soviets had a particular interest in.

Zarubin

As with all their prisoners, the Soviets collected fanatically detailed dossiers on all of the Poles. NKVD photographers took dozens of photographs of each prisoner from slightly different angles. During these sessions, the Soviets tried to keep their prisoners off balance with sudden revelations of information, such as abruptly describing the man's home furnishings and their exact positions in his house.

The Soviets also undertook a zealous if largely unsuccessful political indoctrination program as late February 1940 arrived. They showed a wide range of pro-Russian or pro-Soviet films, including such titles as "Tale of Happiness Hard Won," "Lenin in October," "Peter the First, Parts 1 and 2," "Lenin in 1918," and "Heroes of the Homeland." At the same time, they considerably increased the quality and quantity of food in an effort to win the Poles over to the Bolshevik cause. Other indoctrination efforts included numerous talks and seminars on communist, Marxist, or revolutionary topics, a reading room with newspapers and almost 4,000 selected communist books and tracts, and radio broadcasts thundering out over loudspeakers. A report by Commissar Semyon Nekhoroshev at Starobilsk recommended installing more loudspeakers to increase constant indoctrination efforts: "Expand the radio network in the camp by providing eleven points with loudspeakers (there will be forty-three radio points in all), and provide radio service in the club building by installing five loudspeakers." (Cienciala, 2007, 94).

Someone higher in the system wrote on the margin using red pencil that banning religious observances represented a mistake. Though likely coincidental, it remains interesting to note that Stalin constantly carried a red pencil during the war years, using it to take notes, draw on maps, or simply doodle his favorite picture of wolf's heads.

Regardless, the Poles greeted the bombardment of propaganda with almost total disinterest, though the Commissar could not resist describing the avidity with which they watched movie screenings – perhaps a piece of Soviet propaganda, or perhaps simply the desire of bored, tired, and anxious men for any form of entertainment or escapism. The officers frankly told the Soviets that they wanted the Soviets as allies in the war, but not as masters. They consumed the newspapers and radio broadcasts, attempting to read between the triumphalist Soviet lines to determine the events of the outside world.

Chapter 4: The Decision to Exterminate the Poles

The Soviets' plans for their Polish prisoners did not at first involve their liquidation; in fact, the Russians seemed to have no clear idea what they wished to do with the men. In November 1939, Soviet officials put several proposals forward. One involved putting the Poles to work on road-building on the Lvov Highway, while another would have assigned the men to mining. In each case, they would have taken the place of other POWs, whom the Soviets would have sent home.

These suggestions, however, brought the men to the notice of the sinister Lavrenty Beria, Minister of Internal Affairs of the Soviet Union, Gulag chief, would-be Soviet premier, and prolific rapist. Beria began taking an interest in the Poles as the Soviets continued deciding what to do with them. In February, Pyotr Soprunenko proposed sending home several hundred sick men, along with any prisoners over 60 years of age and several hundred military reservists. Since the "Winter War" with Finland occurred at that time, Soprunenko may have been trying to make room for anticipated Finnish prisoners in his camps. In the event, most of those he listed stayed at the camps and eventually went to their deaths.

After some debate, either not recorded directly or not yet found or made public, the Soviet leadership decided to kill all of the Polish prisoners in the three camps, and approximately 7,000 more held in various NKVD prisons. This decision, reached in the first days of March 1940, apparently derived from the continued nationalist patriotism of the prisoners and their refusal to accept the imperial dominion of communist internationalism. This natural ethnic and national loyalty received the labor of "counterrevolutionary," which it actually was in an objective sense, but it required a Soviet lens to transform that counterrevolutionary loyalty to people and homeland into a crime punishable by death. Lavrenty Beria's memorandum to Stalin dooming the prisoners included the following items: "1) examine the cases of the 14,700 former Polish officers, officials, landowners, police, [...] and prison guards who are now in the prisoner-of-war camps 2) and also examine the cases of those who have been arrested and are in the prisons of the western oblasts of Ukraine and Belorussia, numbering 11,000, [...] former landowners, manufacturers, former Polish officers, [...] [and] using the special procedure, apply to them the supreme punishment, [execution by] shooting." (Cienciela, , 119-120).

Beria

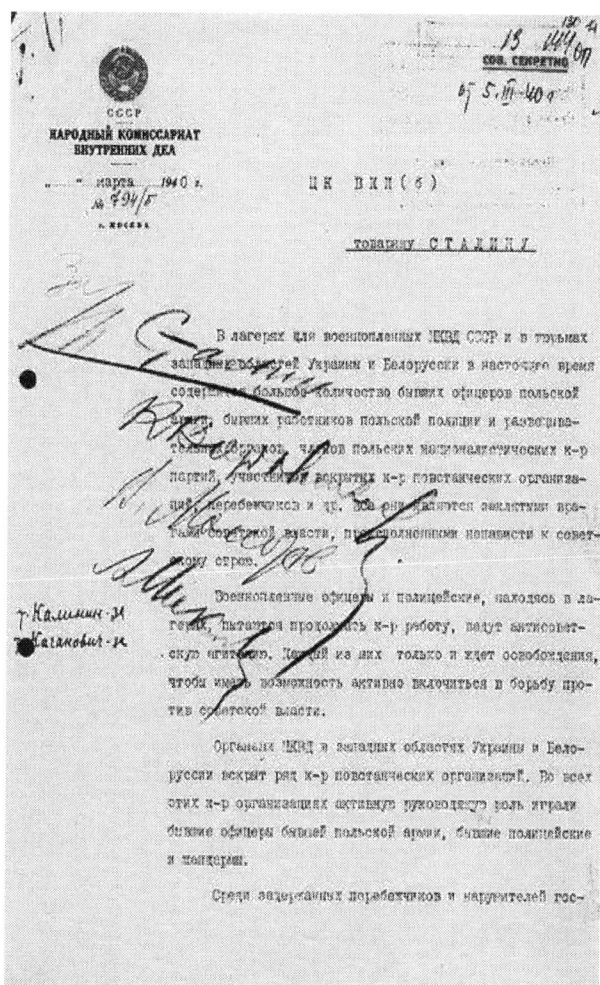

A picture of Beria's memo to Stalin

Though Beria made the suggestion, Stalin held the final power in deciding if the men would die. An unabashed mass murderer who esteemed executioners as cultural heroes rather than the loathed if necessary semi-outcasts they represented through the rest of history, and a sadist reduced to helpless gales of laughter when his court jester Karl Pauker, an ethnic Jew, mockingly imitated the screams and pleas for mercy of people killed by the NKVD, Stalin had no difficulty in sentencing the Poles to execution.

In conjunction with the plan, the Soviets decided to simultaneously deport 22,000-25,000 Polish families to Kazakhstan to for 10 years' hard labor. This, the Soviets calculated, would conceal the crime from the other Poles sufficiently enough to enable them to construct a stable

Marxist state in their region of Poland. These deportations and many others duly took place.

Chapter 5: The Massacre

Though known as the Katyn Forest Massacre or the Katyn Massacre, only part of the mass execution of Polish officers actually occurred there. In all, the Soviets killed an estimated 21,857 Polish prisoners during the interlinked massacres of April 1940, as revealed by a centralized list first brought to light again in 1959. The men at Ostashkov, Kozelsk, and Starobilsk do not add up to this sum, but many thousands of others perished at NKVD jails in Belarus and the Ukraine as well. As many as 7,000 men may have been shot in Minsk, but the Belarusian government of the early 21st century refuses to permit research or archeology on its territory. This remains the most obscure of the early 1940 mass murders of Poles.

The other killings, however, generated eyewitness accounts, and those at Katyn Forest underwent repeated international scrutiny, making them emblematic of the whole slaughter.

The Soviets slated the execution of the men at all three camps to occur simultaneously, though the differing methods used ensured that the killings took place over a slightly different timeframe at each facility. In all cases, the NKVD took the men elsewhere to kill them,

Many decades later, in 1990, the then 89-year-old Vladimir Tokaryev provided a videotaped interview describing the execution of the Poles from Ostashkov, some 6,500 men in all. One man actually pulled the trigger on most of the prisoners, Vasily Blokhin, a square-faced man with a belligerent look who, with this one "project," became the executioner with the most deaths to his name in history and likely became the world's deadliest serial killer in one fell swoop. Approximately 30 other men, probably including Tokaryev despite his repeated denials, also had a hand in the killings.

Throughout the process of execution, the Soviets took extreme care to hide the men's fates from them until the very last moment, in most cases at least. This prevented resistance from the policemen and soldiers who made up the majority of the victims – muscular young men trained in the use of violence, and therefore unlikely to go meekly to their deaths if aware of their coming destruction. Moreover, the killings occurred only at night, except on the first day when Vasily Blokhin carried on killing too long in order to bring his total to 300 men executed for the day, in accordance with a daily quota he set for carrying out the massacre. Blokhin worked for the Cheka, the GPU, and other Soviet secret police bodies for many years prior to his NKVD period, always noted and commended for his bloodthirstiness and willingness to participate in any kind of execution, murder, or torture.

Blokhin

The NKVD transferred the prisoners from Ostashkov to the NKVD prison in Kalinin, where most of the executions took place. There, the Soviets placed the Poles in cells and brought them out one by one to the "Red Corner," the NKVD men's relaxation area. In the first room, NKVD officers asked each man his name and date of birth in order to match him to their list. Then, without providing any more information, the officers indicated the man should enter the second room.

Inside the second room, carefully soundproofed to block all sounds of shooting, an executioner and several NKVD soldiers waited. Blokhin almost always officiated personally, carrying out the executions himself, though the other men also took turns at times, possibly in part to implicate them also. Tokaryev described Blokhin's garb, designed to keep his clothing free of blood and brain matter: "I remember Blokhin saying: 'Come on, let's go.' And then he put on his special uniform for the job: brown leather hat, brown leather apron, long brown leather gloves reaching above the elbows. They were his terrible trademark. I was face to face with a true executioner." (Remnick, 1994, 5-6).

Inside the notorious room, two men would grab the Polish prisoner's arms and hold him while Blokhin (or another man) put a pistol to the base of his skull and fired, shooting at a slight angle so that the bullet emerged from the forehead, precisely as would be the case with the men executed in the forest near Kozy Gorye. The NKVD soldiers then hustled the corpse out to a waiting truck. As that was transpiring, other NKVD men had already selected another Pole from the cells and had began walking him through his final circuit down the hall to the Red Corner and the soundproofed room beyond. In this way, the Soviets kept up a continuous stream of prisoners all night long, enabling the shooting of 250 men per night (and 300 the first night, due to the enthusiasm of Blokhin for his work). This amounted to a shooting every three minutes during the night shift.

The executions started at the beginning of April 1940 and continued for approximately 25 days, occupying nearly the entire month. Blokhin brought a suitcase filled with Walther PPK pistols, freshly manufactured and purchased from the Third Reich, to carry out the executions. His men also supplied large quantities of Geko 7.62mm ammunition, also manufactured in Germany. Blokhin's use of German pistols and ammunition related to quality and technical characteristics, not to any advance plan to "frame" the Germans for the killings. He chose the Walther PPK over the Nagant M1895 revolver due to the latter's tendency to overheat, along with its strong recoil. Far less apt to overheat or jam, the PPK also featured a much lighter recoil, an important consideration for a man about to fire at least 250 shots in one night. The PPK, a semiautomatic, also offered easier loading characteristics and ejected spent shell casings in the manner of other semiautomatic pistols. The M1895, on the other hand, did not eject casings, requiring the user to extract each piece of spent brass individually, a time-consuming and frustrating process. Blokhin used Geko ammunition due to its much higher reliability compared to Soviet cartridges.

Blokhin also made an alcohol ration part of the grim ritual of execution, helping to stiffen the nerve of his NKVD men. Tokaryev explained, "Blokhin made sure that everyone in the execution team got a supply of vodka after each night's work. Every evening he brought it into the prison in boxes. They drank nothing before the shooting or during the shooting, but afterward they all had a few glasses before going home to bed." (Remnick, 1994, 6).

Other NKVD men stacked the corpses in the truck and drove them from Kalinin to a pleasant

Russian open forest near the village of Mednoye, on the north bank of the Tvertsa River. After a drive of about 20 miles, the trucks arrived at a spot fairly close to the NKVD dachas in the area. In fact, Tokaryev's dacha stood closest to the burial site. There, several NKVD men using a bulldozer had excavated a ditch-like mass grave approximately 30 feet long. The men unloaded the corpses from the truck and stacked them neatly in the grave, packing them tightly for maximum efficiency. Once they had cleared the truck, the Russians used the bulldozer to push the earth back over the buried men, creating a long, low mound. The burials at Mednoye remained top secret until the fall of the Soviet Union, with the official Soviet line claiming that all the Polish prisoners underwent execution and burial in the Kozy Gorye (Goat Hills) of Katyn Forest.

A mass grave being unearthed in the Katyn Forest

A simple reason prompted this extraordinary secrecy. The Germans held the Kozy Gorye area for a time during their invasion of Russia, but, although a tank battle occurred near Mednoye, the Wehrmacht never held the town. Thus, any mass burials in the area could only be the responsibility of the Soviet state itself, and the USSR did not want such "open and shut" evidence made known.

Out of the 6,312 men doomed to execution at Kalinin, only one escaped once the killings began. The executioners received an urgent official telephone call from Moscow instructing them not to kill a 2nd Lieutenant in the Polish Army Health Service named Michal Romm. His uncle, a Soviet film director named Mikhail Romm, managed to win him this reprieve. The call arrived only an hour or two before Romm would have met his fate at Blokhin's hands in the Red Corner. The executioners accordingly spared him, and the young Pole survived to become a Soviet citizen and follow his uncle's career path, working as a film director in the USSR.

After completing the butchery, Blokhin and his men received an extra month's wages as a reward from Beria. Blokhin organized a banquet to celebrate the completion of the task. Many decades later, Tokaryev claimed he refused to attend, but such a refusal seems unlikely in the atmosphere of murderous paranoia during the Stalin purge years.

For its part, the killing of the Poles held at Starobilsk camp occurred with considerably less efficiency than the massacres inflicted elsewhere. Those carrying out the executions had between 3,739 and 3,896, depending on the source, half the number at Ostashkov and hundreds less than at Kozelsk. Nevertheless, the NKVD took almost two months, April and May 1940, to dispose of these men.

Documentary evidence regarding the Starobilsk killings remains sketchy, with few details available even after the opening of the Soviet records at the fall of the USSR. Only one known eyewitness account remains extant, that of the former NKVD lieutenant Mitrofan Syromiatnikov. According to Syromiatnikov, the Poles arrived in Kharkov, Ukraine by train in batches of 100, or occasionally 200. After arrival at the station, the NKVD loaded the Poles onto trucks, transporting them to the NKVD prison in town. Syromiatnikov's garbled and contradictory accounts on different occasions indicate the Poles might have been kept in cells for an hour or two, or anywhere up to several days. He claimed that the NKVD provided a cover story for the executions, stating that the men had staged a revolt at their prison and for this reason received a death sentence.

However long the Poles awaited their fate, whether it was for hours or days, their executions showed the same effort to prevent them from knowing of their imminent death in order to prevent them from fighting back. The NKVD men brought the Poles one by one to the Kharkov prison cellar, where Timofei Khupry, the prison chief, and several other NKVD men asked them several identifying questions in order to match them to the list. And in contrast to Blokhin's murderously well-oiled operation, the NKVD at Kharkov used Nagant M1895 revolvers. Syromiatnikov saw one of the other NKVD men laboriously extracting the spent cartridges from half a dozen of these revolvers and reloading them for the next group of executions.

Once the prisoner identified himself, Kupry told him "You may go." (Cienciala, 2007, 129). This constituted the signal to seize the man so that Kupry or another executioner could immediately shoot him in the base of the skull with a Nagant M1895. The NKVD guards wrapped the prisoner's head in his coat just after shooting to contain the bleeding, and then they subsequently carried the body into a nearby room to get it out of sight.

The NKVD men transferred the corpses to a truck parked at a hidden entrance of the prison. Once they fully loaded the truck, the coats still wrapped around the corpses' heads to control bleeding on the truck bed, they drove the vehicle to a forested park near an NKVD summer resort on the northern fringes of Kharkov, in Piatikhatki. There the Soviets placed the Poles' corpses into mass graves and eventually covered over them.

Once the executions finally ended, some 3,800 Poles lay in the Piatikhatki mass graves. Beria sent a reward of 800 rubles to each of the NKVD men who participated in the task, though Syromiatnikov claimed that the prison commander and chief executioner Kupry stole the other men's premiums so that they never actually received them.

Some of the most famous mass graves from the Katyn Massacre lie in the Kozy Gorye, or Goat Hills, near Smolensk. According to the locals, the NKVD and its predecessors the GRU and Cheka used this pleasant wooded area on the north bank of Dnieper River in Smolensk Oblast, just west of the city of Smolensk, as an execution ground for decades. Many Russians and Belarusians also judged to fall short of the communist idea met their deaths in this green riverside "dumping ground."

The Soviets went to great pains to deceive their prisoners into thinking they intended to send them home rather than kill them. In addition to receiving apparently genuine railroad passes and being allowed to pack and bring their suitcases, some of the Soviet measures reached a level of deceptive perfidy perhaps meriting the label of "grotesque." One account from the time claimed, "In order to give a more festive air to the departure, the camp authorities organized a band to play as the convoys left. This produced an excellent effect on the prisoners." (Cienciala, 2007, 123).

This brass band sendoff did not represent the sole Soviet attempt to lull the suspicions of their captives immediately before their execution. Some of the most vivid accounts come from the Polish professor Swianiewicz, who was actually placed on an execution train that traveled to the Katyn Forest but was spared, like Michal Romm, by behind-the-scenes intervention at the last moment. According to Swianiewicz, "March, 1940 was a joyful month in the Kozielsk camp. From the surrounding fields and forests came the breath of spring. Deep snow still covered the ground but spring was in the air. The nights were still very cold but the pure, frosty air acted like a tonic while the aromas of awakening nature caressed the senses. […] There were several reasons for the sense of joyful anticipation pervading the camp." (FitzGibbon, 1971, 54).

Many of the Poles merely expected to be transferred to German custody for the rest of the war, but this would at least bring them closer to Poland and might offer opportunities to see their families while being transported west. However, in early March, a tall, powerfully built NKVD officer with a brutal-looking "ruddy-purplish" face visited the Kozelsk camp, a man the Poles had not seen before and who made no effort to speak to them. He toured the camp silently, observing everything before taking his leave. This may have been Major-General Pyotr

Soprunenko, who organized the operation at all levels for Beria.

Weeks later, on April 3rd, the Soviets began taking away trainloads of Poles from Kozelsk. Each group received a dinner of good quality before leaving, the best they had eaten since being taken prisoner. None of the men seemed to realize this represented a last meal. As they boarded the train, the Russians gave each man a two-pound loaf of fresh bread, a packet of sugar, and three herrings wrapped in gray paper.

The Poles in the camp saw each group off with immense cheering in addition to the efforts of the band, along with many good wishes and requests to bring word to families if they in fact found themselves sent home. Swianiewicz noted this solidarity, and the fact that there "was not the slightest suspicion that this unification was taking place in the shadow of Lady Death – who unites and levels all, who weaves her somber background to the colorful highlights of life and has a special affection for soldiers in times of war." (FitzGibbon, 1971, 59).

Each morning, Moscow telephoned with a list of 300 more men to be sent off. Of all the groups, only one with 107 men on board would survive. This small trainload received a different destination than the Katyn Forest, spared for reasons that seem impenetrable even to this day. These soldiers left on April 26th, and Lieutenant W.J. Furtek later said that the selection appeared random even to the camp commissar Demidovich, who remarked to the men, "Nu, tak vy horosho popali" (roughly equivalent to "Well, how you've lucked out!"). The Poles initially thought he spoke ironically.

The rest, far from being sent home to their families, instead traveled by rail to a dead-end siding at Gnezdovo Station, just west of Smolensk on the upper Dnieper River. There the NKVD took the men several miles into the Katyn Forest to the Kozy Gorye, shot them in the head, and stacked the corpses in dense piles several yards deep in mass graves. This site differed from the others in one important regard: the Germans discovered it during their subsequent invasion of the Soviet Union and brought it to the world's attention.

Initially, at least, the Soviets apparently tried to execute the Poles by shooting them at the edge of a prepared grave, allowing the corpses to tumble in following the volley. Some mass graves showed jumbled, disordered corpses characteristic of such a technique. However, Tokaryev, who also knew many of the details of the other massacres, spoke disparagingly of the initial arrangements at Katyn Forest, where he referred to "a more stupid procedure. There they began to shoot [the prisoners] at the burial site." (Cienciala, 2007, 125).

Some of the bodies show what Tokaryev referred to when he spoke of "stupidity." These bodies, jumbled in disorder, evidently came from men shot at the edge of a grave. That they knew of their fate and tried to resist it emerges clearly from the condition of these corpses during the 1943 excavations. The Soviets had packed their mouths full of sawdust, then pulled their jackets up over their heads or placed a hood over them. A noose then went around the man's neck, connected to bindings on his wrists so that if he struggled, he would strangle himself. The Soviets used sections of natural cord (without dye) pre-cut to exact lengths, showing they had expected such an eventuality and that the cords did not represent a completely ad hoc solution. In some cases, the Soviets tied the Poles so tightly that the cords sliced into their flesh.

The NKVD men then shot the prisoners and allowed their bodies to roll down into the mass graves. These elaborately brutal preparations show that the Poles had realized their fate, attempted to escape or attack the men designated to shoot them, and required extraordinary measures to subdue them long enough for the executions to take place. A handful of these men bore deep bayonet stab wounds in their bodies from four-sided Soviet bayonets, probably due to their continuing to fight desperately even after being bound. A few also had shattered jaws, probably broken by a blow from a rifle butt while subduing them. This clearly represents what Tokarev considered "stupidity" – showing the prisoners the grave before killing them, thus prompting them to fight, possibly even injuring some of the NKVD men in the process. With nothing to lose and a grave floored with corpses ahead of them, the Poles chose to "go down fighting," compelling the Soviets to half-stifle them with sawdust and tie them in a manner preventing resistance in order to complete their grim work.

After these initial burials – those in the so-called "Grave #5" – the NKVD switched their tactics. In some manner, they managed to execute large numbers of men in a short amount of time without arousing their suspicions, and without producing any noise of gunfire. People living in the area and other witnesses close by reported silence, with no gunshots most of the time, yet medical examination of the corpses showed that Soviets shot all the men in such a way that the bullets traveled from the base of the skull to punch out through the forehead.

An almost ghostly quality hangs over the Katyn Forest executions at the Gnezdovo Station. Polish witnesses who remained on the train due to orders individually sparing them saw the other men, alive and not bound, disembarking after pulling into the dead end siding at Gnezdovo. The men then boarded either "Chyornaye voron" – "black raven" or "carrion crow" cars, the characteristic black cars used by the NKVD – or buses with the windows coated in powdered chalk. From there, the Soviets took them into the forest. At some point before reaching the mass graves, the NKVD men killed their prisoners in such a way that the large numbers waiting a short distance away near the train heard nothing. They then laid the corpses neatly in the graves, stacking them carefully to maximize the capacity of each burial site. The men died without being bound, meaning they had no inkling of their impending death until the moment an NKVD man pulled the trigger.

How the Soviets managed this puzzled the Germans investigating in 1943 and subsequent investigators also. The Germans examined a nearby garage, but they found no empty shell casings there. Additionally, the burial pits themselves contain only a small scattering of shell casings, though the outdoor setting would have made retrieval of so much "brass" nearly impossible. The men, therefore, did not suffer execution on the train, in the garage near the graves, or at the graves themselves, though earlier accounts of the Katyn Massacre incorrectly "reconstruct" the Soviets shooting the Poles while they knelt, bound, on the edge of the graves. Neither forensic evidence nor the archaeological evidence of spent brass supports this description, despite its frequent inclusion as a fact in books about Katyn.

Nevertheless, the graves yielded two pieces of evidence hinting at the truth – a pair of brief, furtively kept diary entries found later on documents in the clothing of several corpses in the mass burials. The diary of Major Adam Solski represents the eeriest piece of Katyn evidence, since the Major seemingly continued writing until a few moments before the NKVD killed him. His entry reads: "9.04. Five a.m. The day began in a special way at dawn. Departure in a prison car in cells (awful!). We were driven to some place in a wood; something like a summer resort. Here, a detailed search took place. They took my watch, showing 6:30. They asked about my wedding ring. [...] They took rubles, main belt, penknife." (Cienciala, 2007, 130).

Solski's last observation about a "summer resort" could only have been written minutes before a bullet went through his skull and ended his life. The fact that the NKVD men looted him of his last possessions also indicated the imminence of his death and burial. A second textual fragment from a few days later, almost indecipherable, read, "5hrs. 5[?] km past Smolensk, there is a summer resort [?] 127[?] people." (Cienciala, 2007, 130).

The double mention of a summer resort seems unlikely to be a coincidence, and in fact at that time an NKVD summer woodland resort stood in the Katyn Forest not too far removed from the burial site. The Germans called this structure the "Schlösschen," or "Little Castle," or the "GPU-Erholungsheim," or "GPU Health Resort." A map prepared by one of the German investigators after the war shows this resort quite close to the Dnieper River, though it later burned down.

Local rumors stated that 50 NKVD men from Minsk, Belarus formed the execution squad. Though no direct evidence survives, it seems likely that these men executed the Poles at the summer resort, probably in a similar manner to Blokhin's executions. The men could be brought one by one to a cellar or interior room, shot by surprise, and have their body quickly removed to make place for the next victim. This would explain the lack of audible gunshots and of cartridge cases, which could be easily collected inside.

A Russian, Ivan Krivozertsev (whose name literally means "John Crooked-Heart"), provided extensive depositions regarding the Koze Gory (Goat Hills) shootings. Krivozertsev eventually managed to flee to England along with Polish refugees from the Soviet regime, though he apparently hanged himself in mysterious circumstances in 1947 in a Somerset orchard. Suspicion that an NKVD death squad surreptitiously entered England and assassinated him to keep the secret of Katyn has existed for decades, despite a lack of proof. The British police proved extremely reluctant to speak of his death to allied Polish officers inquiring as to his whereabouts.

Krivozertsev, testifying to Major Stanisław Rodziewicz in London on July 27th, 1946, described how the Soviets pretended that the mass graves actually represented building sites when using local convicts to prepare them: "At the beginning of March 1940 it was rumoured that the *NKVD* would be erecting some buildings in the forest in Koze Gory as the ground was being excavated for foundations. These were dug by the civilian prisoners, brought there from prison in Smolensk, in three or four lorries under *NKVD* guard. [...] This work was started at the beginning of March." (Maresch, 2010, 21). The Soviet deception involved spreading disinformation even to prisoners completely under their control. The Katyn Massacre would be concealed to the utmost so that the Poles would, hopefully, simply vanish and their memory would fade following the deportation of their families to remote locations.

Krivozertsev's invaluable testimony went on to corroborate that the Poles arrived in batches by train, followed by their transfer to waiting cars, with their luggage thrown in a military truck. Some people seeing the Poles arrive believed that the Soviets placed them in a new POW camp. However, Krivozertsev noted that no new road-building occurred, as almost always happened near POW camps. He also reported, "A relative of mine told me that when the wagons with the officers were shunted to the blind-siding; he had seen among the escort an *NKVD* man of his acquaintance. He started talking with him and asked him whether these officers were being transferred to camps. This man replied: 'And where are these camps here? Why do you talk such nonsense, don't you know where they take such people?.'" (Maresch, 2010, 21).

The NKVD men laid all the bodies face-down with their arms at their sides and their legs stretched out, stacking them densely to maximize the number in each grave. Once they executed the last group of 50 Poles on May 12, 1940, the Soviets filled in and leveled the graves to conceal them. They planted two year old spruce saplings on the graves to further obscure their outlines. After that, the NKVD maintained fences around the area and guard patrols with German shepherd dogs to keep the local people from stumbling across the secret.

Chapter 6: The Discovery of the Massacre

Despite the elaborate lengths the Soviets went to in order to conceal their crimes, inquiries about the fate of the men began almost immediately. Initially, the Soviets stated that the men had all been released to return home, but this obviously represented a falsehood because the men had not reached Poland. Soon the Soviet government changed the story to suggest that they had no idea themselves of what had become of the Poles. After that, the official line focused on a bizarre, even risible assertion that the Poles had fled into the puppet state of Manchuria that the Japanese had carved out of northeastern China. Eventually, they stopped responding entirely to queries from either Polish individuals in Poland or the representatives of other governments.

In the meantime, the NKVD relocated the approximately 400 Poles spared from the three camps to a new, fourth camp, Pavlishchev Bor. This camp, located in pine-dotted parkland, proved more spacious and better-constructed than the ad hoc camps used to house the Poles up until this time. Most of the men placed at Pavlishchev Bor survived to either join the communist Polish army units formed in the Soviet Union or eventually be sent home to Poland.

After the Germans took the Smolensk area in summer 1941 during the first days of Operation Barbarossa, the secret of the Katyn Forest Massacre remained undiscovered for some time. The Soviets covered their tracks well, concealing the graves, terrorizing the local people into silence, arresting some of those they thought knew too much, and deporting the victims' families to the ghastly camps of Kazakhstan to eliminate those who might inquire about the men's whereabouts. As a result, the Katyn Massacre only came to light as a result of German war efforts using Polish prisoners as workers. Smolensk, the scene of extensive, vicious fighting during the advance into the Soviet Union in summer 1941, represented a rich source of scavenged metal, such as scrap iron and scrap steel. The German military engineering organization, the Todt Organization (named for its founder Fritz Todt), sent Polish prisoners into the area to comb the landscape for salvageable metal to send back to Germany's war industry.

The Poles working near the Kozy Gorye spoke with the local people, who informed them of mass graves holding Polish officers in the Goat Hills forest. The Poles, startled by this information, probed further, and found a local man, Parfeon Kisilev, who could take them to the exact spot. He led them into the Katyn Forest to a place where seven large graves could be seen, with young pine trees planted on top of them. The Polish prisoners made a small wooden cross and erected it near the graves in memory of their slain countrymen, but the Germans did not take an immediate interest in the matter. Instead, they mentioned in an article in their Russian language "Noviy Put" ("New Way") newspaper in early 1943 that General Sikorski could not determine what had happened to thousands of Polish officers captured by the Soviets in 1939.

Ivan Krivozertsov brought this article to the attention of a locally stationed *Geheim Feldpolizei* (Wehrmacht Gestapo) officer, and told him of the rumored burials in the Katyn Forest. The following day, Friedrich Ahrens and other Gestapo men drove to the forest on motorcycles, with Krivozertsov and several other locals coming along in a cart. Since they could not locate the graves, they sought out Parfeon Kisilev, whom they found trying to hide in an alcove just above the large ceramic stove in his house.

Kisilev brought the men to the burial site, where the Germans ordered Krivozertsov, another man, and Kisilev to start digging into one of the graves, as Krivozertsov described: "We first broke up the frozen soil with pickaxes and then started digging with shovels. After we dug a fairly deep hole, there arose a smell of decay. As my two colleagues could not bear this smell [...] I [...] was left alone to dig to the end. We were digging up sand the whole time and at the bottom of the pit, there was a thin layer of darkened soil under which lay the corpses. I saw a military grey coat and short belt at the back, because the corpses lay face downwards." (Maresch, 2010, 21).

The Germans halted the initial excavation at this point with one button bearing the eagle of the

Polish army in their possession. The exhumation resumed when Leutnant Ludwig Voss of the Wehrmacht Gestapo arrived along with interpreters and other personnel. Voss had the hole widened and a corpse's head brought to him, presumably to confirm death by shooting. Then he ordered the earth put back in the hole, probably to preserve the crime scene for Red Cross witnessing.

The Germans began to question the people in the area about the situation, gathering information they could use in denouncing the Soviets in the hopes of driving a wedge between the eastern and western Allies. The Austrian interpreter and Unteroffizier Gustav Ponka headed this commission of inquiry. Ponka had no need to use coercive methods to get the people to speak, since none of the people showed reticence in freely reporting what they had seen, operating under the erroneous belief that the Soviets would never return.

The Russian peasants in the area confirmed at the time to the Red Cross, and later to their Western interrogators if they managed to escape to Western Europe, that the Germans had used the "NKVD summer resort," but only in small numbers. They never saw more than a single car arrive bearing an officer taking a brief holiday from the front. This testimony, along with the other masses of evidence, helped to establish that the Germans had not committed this particular massacre. The peasants also noted that the Germans allowed them to disassemble the wooden fence the NKVD placed around the Koziy Gorye, and to move freely through the woods in search of mushrooms in the manner of Russians from time immemorial. Kisilev likely found the graves initially during one of these expeditions.

The Koziy Gorye area had been a favorite Soviet spot for mass executions since 1918, according to the local inhabitants. The Cheka, GRU, and NKVD successively brought numbers of people to the area who never left. In fact, the subsequent investigations by the Red Cross and the Germans found a number of older graves containing thousands of skeletons. Many of these burial areas had become quite overgrown in the years since their creation, and some undoubtedly escaped detection due to fully blending into the natural landscape under trees, grass, and underbrush.

The Germans excavated only enough to prove the presence of numerous corpses, then refilled many of the graves to preserve the evidence for outside observers to see. They took core samples from the suspected gravesites, bringing up scraps of uniform cloth, pieces of compressed and partially mummified flesh, and adipocere from multiple locations, revealing an extensive area of mass graves. After this, the Third Reich invited various international groups to examine the mass graves in order to establish them as a Soviet war crime. The Germans, of course, hoped that this would cause dissent among the Allies, possibly even a split, though ultimately the Western Allies merely shrugged and the Soviets issued strident denials.

A mass grave unearthed in the Katyn Forest

A picture of Polish items found in the mass graves

The Polish Red Cross and the International Medical Commission both sent teams to the Katyn Forest site. Though invited, the International Red Cross itself declined to send any personnel to the area due to the fact that the Soviet Union had not requested their presence. The International Medical Commission consisted of 12 doctors specializing in forensic medicine and criminology, sent from a range of European universities. The commissioners noted that the Germans and international experts exhumed 982 bodies by April 30, 1943, and further exhumations followed.

The Commission noted several details not mentioned in other sources, such as the fact that the Soviets turned all the Polish collars up and shot them through the collar, rather than with the pistol muzzle in direct contact with the victim's head. In some cases, the shell casing, upon ejection, landed between the Pole's neck and his upturned collar and, trapped there, underwent burial along with him. There were other facts noted: "That the shots had been fired from a barrel touching the nape of the neck or at extremely close range is proved by the cracks in the skull, by traces of gunpowder on the base of the skull close to the entrance of the bullet [...] The striking uniformity of the injuries and the position of the bullet's entry, all within a very small circumference on the lower part of the skull, point to experienced hands having been at work."

The Commission noted that while many Poles died from a single pistol shot, others succumbed to two or even three shots delivered to the base of the skull very close together. In one extraordinary case, one Polish skull bore a bullet embedded in the bone at the side, indicating that the NKVD shot another man simultaneously and the round struck the second man with most of its force expended after punching through the primary victim's skull. This suggested the Soviets might have shot at least some Poles in groups.

The Commission doctors, in establishing "time of death," noted that no insects appeared on the corpses, indicating their burial in the cooler months. In warmer weather, flies and other insects would have covered the corpses and been interred with the men once the Soviets bulldozed the graves shut.

The men towards the outer edges appeared mummified, while those in the middle of the mass had exuded large amounts of adipocere or "grave wax," clumping them together in a mass. In an effort to establish how long ago they had died, the men performed autopsies on a number of skulls. The brain matter had turned to a clay-like necrotic substance, which, the doctors asserted, could not happen in less than two years and likely indicated the men had been in the grave for approximately three years.

Further investigation revealed large numbers of documents in the corpses' pockets, including sections of Polish and Russian newspaper along with diaries, letters, paper money, Polish passports, and other material. In many cases the items clumped together in sticky masses of adipocere, requiring painstaking cleaning in special chemical baths for restoration. The commissioners could find no documents dated later than April 22, 1940.

Besides the various foreign doctors given access to the site by the Germans in spring 1943, the Nazis also brought a group of unwilling British, American, and Commonwealth prisoners of war to Katyn in order to witness the exhumation. One of these men, U.S. Army Lieutenant Donald Stewart, provided detailed testimony after his liberation by the Fourth Armored Division in April

1945. These men arrived with the preconceived idea that the Germans committed the massacre and now attempted to blame the Soviets. However, they left convinced that the Soviets in fact represented the guilty parties, though none admitted it at the time to the Germans and only revealed their conclusions after the war. Stewart professed absolute hatred for the Germans, citing this as a reason he would not be inclined toward a reading of the situation in their favor.

Picture of a group of Allied POWs taken to Katyn to witness exhumations

The eight prisoners of war, four officers, three enlisted men, and a British civilian, followed a complicated itinerary to reach Katyn Forest. Leaving the Rotenberg camp by train, the men soon reached Kassel, where the British general Fortune had meant to join them. Instead of Fortune, a Scottish medical officer, Captain Stanley Gilder, joined the party. Other members included the British South African Lieutenant Colonel Stevenson, U.S. Lieutenant Colonel John van Vliet, and a German-American translator who identified himself only as "von Johnson."

From Kassel, the Germans put the men on trains for Berlin. The prisoners reached Berlin at dawn on April 11, 1943, where they took an airplane at Templehof Airfield. The German aircraft flew at an altitude of 200 to 300 feet for the entire distance, mostly following railroad tracks. The aircraft set down twice to refuel, first at Breslau and then at Biela-Podlacka, where the Germans served a lunch of hard-boiled eggs, soup, and bread.

On April 12, the Germans drove the POWs to Katyn from Smolensk. The British and Americans, seeing the Germans taking photos and films near the graves, worried that they might be involved in a pure propaganda effort. The Germans showed the prisoners the graves and allowed them to climb down into them. Stewart counted the stacks and rows of corpses in the largest, L-shaped grave and estimated the burials held 9,000-10,000 men.

The Germans showed the prisoners several corpses in the process of autopsy, the contents of their pockets, and the details of their uniforms. They also called Stewart's attention to a curious item seldom mentioned in later accounts: "There was a tree there that had possibly a dozen bullets embedded in it. The German officer went over and put his head against the tree and put his hand up behind it to indicate that very probably the persons that had done the killing had made a man lean his head against the tree and then shot him. One of the officers said it could very well have been just somebody doing target practice." (Madden, 1952, 13).

Stewart testified that he believed the corpses to be several years old due to their condition. Some appeared mummified, while others appeared compressed, black, and hard, covered in a layer of greasy yellow adipocere. Since the Germans had held the area all the way back to 1941, this did not constitute conclusive proof to Stewart's mind that the Soviets carried out the massacre, but his keen powers of observation picked out a detail that the Germans did not point out, and one which convinced him that the Soviets killed the Poles: "[T]he thing that struck us […] was the fact that many of those bodies […] were in overcoats and in good condition; Polish overcoats. We saw several hundred bodies of the Polish officers in uniforms of very good quality that had not been worn. […] The boots were not worn at all; very little wear on them. […] They were less worn than the heels on my shoes right now." (Madden, 1952, 15).

Stewart knew from personal experience that uniforms worn during captivity soon grew heavily battered and worn due to constant use and lack of upkeep. The Poles' uniforms, fresh and new, could not have been worn very long after their capture in 1939. Tailor-fitted, they clearly belonged to the men who wore them and could not have been planted evidence. Since no Poles wore such uniforms since 1939, and the Germans did not hold the Katyn area until late 1941, Stewart reasoned correctly that the men had been shot within a few months of their capture in 1939, and thus could only be victims of the Soviets. Stewart and the others refused to share their conclusions with the Germans, however, and only provided testimony after being freed at the end of the war.

Les mŕtvych v **Katyne**

A picture of a Nazi propaganda poster shining light on the Soviet massacre

The Germans delivered what they hoped would be their bombshell on April 13, 1943, immediately after bringing the 8 Western Allied POWs to view the site. They broadcast the news internationally in a radio statement heard in London, elsewhere in England, and the United States. However, both Churchill and Roosevelt did their best to minimize the news, despite the efforts of the Polish government in exile to call for a full and immediate investigation.

Not surprisingly, the Soviets did not respond immediately to the German statements. When they did, they offered the first of several versions of events before they decided that the best answer of all consisted of stony silence: "The Polish prisoners in question were interned in the vicinity of Smolensk in special camps and were employed in road construction. It was impossible to evacuate them at the time [...] If, therefore, they have been found murdered, it means that they have been murdered by the Germans who, for reasons of provocation, now claim the crime was committed by Soviet authorities." (Pitt, 1972, 1235).

Of course, no camps existed anywhere in the vicinity, nor had prisoners built new roads, both facts confirmed by numerous aerial photographs in addition to Red Cross and local peasant testimony. The Soviets later changed their story, claiming outlandishly that the Germans had brought thousands of corpses and dressed them in Polish Army uniforms – an essentially impossible task with thousands of badly decayed cadavers. Moreover, the Red Cross noted that the uniforms mostly showed a superbly tailored fit to the dead men wearing them, rendering the idea of the Germans dressing Soviet casualties up to simulate a massacre even more absurd. Since many of the men belonged to the officer corps or affluent professions, their undergarments also proved to be individually tailored in many cases.

The Germans contacted both the International Red Cross in Switzerland and the Polish Red Cross with an invitation to visit the Katyn Forest and participate in the exhumation of the bodies. While the Polish Red Cross agreed, the International Red Cross sent back a standard reply, indicating that they would only send representatives if the Soviets also issued them an invitation to investigate and declaring themselves "prepared to give assistance by selecting neutral experts, *on the condition that similar appeals were received from all parties interested in this question.*" (Zawodny, 1962, 33). The International Red Cross could not, by its very rules, comply with the German invitation unless a Soviet invitation also accompanied it. Naturally, Stalin's government made no effort to ask the IRC to investigate, since such efforts could only reveal the truth that the NKVD carried out the butchery.

Instead, the Soviets mounted a frenzied verbal offensive against the Poles as their best defense against the accusations. With almost transcendent hypocrisy, the actual murderers of the Katyn Poles accused the Poles of colluding with the Nazis – or "Hitlerites" as they termed the Germans, to avoid referring to them as "socialists" in any capacity – in an outlandish plot in which the Germans slaughtered the Poles and the Poles blamed the Soviets. Continuing their ostentatious bellowing of injured righteousness, the Soviets broke off all diplomatic relations with the Sikorski government in London. This, of course, left them with the position that the only legitimate government for Poland consisted of their own communist Polish government in exile, filled to the brim with Stalinist stooges. The Soviet foreign minister Vyacheslav Molotov crowned this effort with a statement which claimed the Poles only issued their accusations in an attempt to seize territory from the Soviet Union: "The Soviet government are aware that this hostile campaign against the Soviet Union has been undertaken by the Polish government in order to exert pressure…for the purpose of wresting from them territorial concessions at the expense of the interests of the Soviet Ukraine, Soviet Belorussia and Soviet Lithuania." (Rees, 2010, 185). The areas he named were, in fact, regions seized from Poland by the Soviet Union at the time of the latter's 1939 invasion.

Additionally, Molotov signed the execution order for the Poles directly below Stalin, so his pretense of injured innocence rang particularly hollow. Nevertheless, Churchill's government accepted Molotov's blustering at face value, despite the fact that Churchill and his top officials recognized the Soviets' responsibility privately. Put simply, political expediency overrode every other consideration. Churchill wrote to Stalin, promising to "silence" the Polish press in England as much as possible, though he did make a few half-hearted statements in support of the government in exile. The Allied approach, however, remained that of solemnly backing the falsehoods of the Soviet Union and attempting to quash dissenting voices in order to keep the pressure on Germany. Above all, Churchill and Roosevelt strove to keep the public from learning the true character of the Soviets, for whose assistance their governments asked them to make huge sacrifices of money, effort, and blood.

Even as that effort went on, Sir Owen O'Malley, British ambassador to the Polish government in exile, meticulously demolished all Soviet claims in a series of memorandums sent to Churchill and his cabinet. O'Malley answered each point and refuted it thoroughly, and in conclusion he wrote a bitter summary of the situation: "We have in fact perforce used the good name of England like the murderers used the little conifers to cover up a massacre; and in view of the immense importance of an appearance and of the heroic resistance of Russia to Germany, few will think that any other course would have been wise or right." (Rees, 2010, 188).

O'Malley had no alternative to suggest. After some debate, in which the British Foreign Minister Sir Anthony Eden urged Churchill to suppress the O'Malley report and not send it to President Roosevelt, the Prime Minister nevertheless reluctantly forwarded the document to White House. Roosevelt received a copy but never even bothered to comment on it or acknowledge that it existed. His burning desire for a friendship with Stalin and the influence of such communist dupes or agents as Alger Hiss, along with his own unshakeable certitude, compelled him to disregard O'Malley's densely reasoned and poignantly questioning document entirely.

When the Soviet counteroffensive began to roll towards the Smolensk region in summer of 1943, the peasants who had testified about the Katyn Massacre took flight to the west with retreating German units. They knew the Soviets would imprison or kill them as revenge for speaking of the massacre or at least to prevent them from offering further testimony. Ivan Krivozertsov received help from a German traffic policeman, who flagged down a car full of retreating Germans and added the Russian to the passengers. Another man who testified, the 44-year old Ivan Andreyev (nicknamed "Shlopechka" or "Little Hat"), found himself thrown out of his house by his wife, who thus hoped to keep the home while avoiding retribution from the Soviets. Another man named Ivan Andreyev, this one nicknamed "Rumba" (also the Russian name for the Cuban rumba musical style), also fled in a German car, while Kisilev, the older man who found the graves initially, left on foot with his wife, pushing a wheelbarrow stacked with such of their possessions as he could save. As of September 24, 1943, he remained on the road, fleeing westwards towards Germany, but he could not escape in time under his own power. The NKVD arrested him and his son and, under threat of immediate shooting, Kisilev proclaimed that the Germans compelled him to give false testimony.

After retaking the Katyn Forest region, the Soviets sent their own commission to the site to exhume the corpses once again. This commission barred the presence of any foreigners, including both Red Cross representatives and even the Polish communists, who expressed an interest in participating. The Soviet expedition's level of impartiality appeared in its long-winded title: *"The Special Commission for Ascertaining and Investigating the Circumstances of the Shooting of Polish Officer Prisoners by the German-Fascist Invaders in the Katyn Forest."* Hitler's propaganda minister, Joseph Goebbels, anticipated the outcome of losing the forest to the Soviets again, though this scarcely required prescience: "Unfortunately we have had to give up Katyn. The Bolsheviks undoubtedly will soon 'find' that we shot 12,000 Polish officers. That episode is one that is going to cause us quite a little trouble in the future." (Zawodny, 1962, 49).

The Special Commission traveled to Katyn and exhumed the unfortunate Poles yet again. The President of the Soviet Academy of Medical Science, Nikolai Burdenko, oversaw the proceedings. The NVKD terrorized those peasant witnesses who had not managed to escape into recanting their testimony, after which most secured their release. A few, however, remained in gulags for up to 10 years for the "crime" of stating that the NKVD killed the Polish troops at Katyn.

A stamp depicting Burdenko

The investigation lasted five months, and the NKVD carefully stage-managed a visit by foreign journalists. The Russians included the daughter of ambassador Averell Harriman, Kathleen Harriman, among the party. Upon their arrival, the Russians treated Kathleen Harriman to a display seemingly intended to shock her and probably divert attention from any type of genuine inquiry: "[T]he party went into one of four large gray-green tents, clumping the snow and muck off their boots as they entered. It was warmer inside and the stench was overpowering. Dr. Prozorovsky ripped open a corpse numbered 808, sliced chunks off the brain like cold meat, knifed through the chest and pulled out an atrophied organ. 'Heart,' he said, holding it out to Kathy [Miss Harriman]. Then he slit a leg muscle. 'Look how well preserved the meat is,' he said." (Zawodny, 1962, 53).

The Soviet display failed to cause Kathleen Harriman to blanch, however, and the attempted diversion – if it represented one – failed thoroughly. The reporters began peppering the Soviets with questions, for which the NKVD men appeared totally unprepared. The atmosphere grew intensely hostile as the reporters continued their barrage of suspicious queries, until the Soviets abruptly declared the visit at an end and hustled the Westerners back aboard their train immediately.

Nevertheless, Kathleen Harriman and others stated they believed the Soviet claims overall. At the same time, paradoxically, they stated the Soviet account presented a mass of contradictions and that the Russians presented only flimsy, incomplete evidence. Many people at the time, including prominent British and American politicians, accused Kathleen Harriman and the reporters of saying what the State Department instructed them to say, which they all naturally denied. The Soviets also claimed that the men had material on them dating to December 1941, yet they never produced one of these documents, which could have proven the whole German accusation false.

After the Soviets issued their fabricated report, Churchill asked O'Malley to report on this as well. Once again, O'Malley convincingly demolished the Soviet account point by point. In the United States, the exuberant and life-loving George Howard Earle III, special emissary to the Balkans for Roosevelt, investigated Katyn and prepared his own detailed conclusions. Before he took these to the White House, his friend from the *New York Times*, Joseph Levy, warned, "George, you do not know what you are going to get over there [in the White House]. Harry Hopkins has complete domination over the President and the whole atmosphere over there is 'pink.'" (Rees, 2010, 248).

Earle III

Earle nevertheless went and presented his findings to Roosevelt, who brushed them off and blamed the Germans for the massacre. A few months later, Earle decided to publish his Katyn findings but made the error of first asking Roosevelt's permission. His answer came in the form of a boatload of FBI men who accosted him while he fished from his own boat on a peaceful Maryland lake. The FBI agents bore a letter appointing Earle the assistant chief of the Samoan Defense Group, with orders to leave for Samoa immediately. Bundled out of the United States the same day, Earle spent the rest of the war in Samoa, unable to publish the findings until after the death of Roosevelt and his eventual return to the United States.

Despite all the investigations and accusations, the Soviets maintained their position that the Germans committed the Katyn Massacre for 50 years after the last shot was fired at Kozy Gorye. Though a trickle of details continued to emerge, no absolute certainties existed until the fall of the Soviet Union. All that time, internal documentation inside the USSR, including the execution orders and reports, continued to exist, and some debate continued as to its usefulness. One of the earliest damning communications within the Soviet records following the massacre consists of a letter sent to Nikita Khrushchev by the KGB Chairman A. Shelepin in 1959. In this missive, the KGB Chairman proposes that Khrushchev order the burning of "the records and other documents relating to the shooting of 21,857 Polish officers, gendarmes, police, settlers, and others in 1940 [...] None of these files are of any operational interest to Soviet agencies, nor are they of historical value [...] On the contrary, some unforeseen event might lead to the exposure of the operation [...] Especially as the official version on the shooting of the Poles in Katyn forest is that it was done by the German Fascist invaders." (Volkogonov, 1998, 220).

This document provides a useful total number for the number of men killed during the interlinked massacres of which the Katyn Forest massacre represented one part. However, despite Shelepin's urging, Khrushchev decided to keep the papers intact, and in doing so, he preserved an invaluable historical record of the 1940 killings.

With the 50th anniversary of the massacre approaching and the Soviet Union faltering badly in 1989, the then-head of the KGB, Vladimir Kryuchkov, broached the subject with the Politboro and Mikhail Gorbachev. Kryuchkov and several others argued persuasively that revealing the truth would clear the air and permit the Russians and Poles to move forward in a more amicable fashion: "Apparently we cannot avoid an explanation to [...] Polish society about the tragic affairs of the past. In this instance time is not on our side. Perhaps it would be advisable to say how it really was and who is concretely to blame for what occurred, and with that to close the question. In the final accounting, the costs of such an action will be smaller than the losses we are accumulating from our current inactivity." (Tumarkin, 1994, 180-181).

Kryuchkov

Accordingly, Gorbachev turned over copies of the documents to Wojciech Jaruzelski on April 13, 1990. Interestingly, he chose the 47th anniversary of Goebbels' announcement of the Katyn Massacre discovery by the Germans as the date on which to admit that the NKVD killed the Polish prisoners. The Russians made a feeble effort to prosecute a few of the men involved in the massacre who remained alive, though key figures such as Blokhin died in the 1950s – possibly conveniently, since Stalin's favorite executioner perished, allegedly as a suicide, just two years after Stalin himself died.

Gorbachev and President Bush in 1990

However, even in those cases brought to court, the men involved proved so feeble, ancient, and often mostly blind that the judges dismissed the cases rather than pursuing them to the end. For example, the case of Soprunenko, who may have been the man with the "butcher's face" touring Kozelsk immediately before the start of the executions, was emblematic of what happened: "In 1991 the USSR Chief Military Prosecutor began to take action against Soprunenko for his part in the massacre of 6,000 Polish POW officers from the Ostashkov camp. At 83, nearly blind and recovering from a cancer operation, Soprunenko was using a Kaltenbrunner Defense (denying his own signature, etc.) during interrogations." (Parrish, 1996, 325).

In other cases, the men charged simply declared they had done nothing except stand by in horror, and with such a remove of time, proving otherwise seemed impossible. The Poles investigated the grave sites after half a century of doubt and uncertainty, and striking memorials now stand at both the Kozy Gorye and Mednoye around the low mounds where some 22,000 Polish soldiers and policemen lie beside tens of thousands of Russians killed at the behest of Stalin and Beria during the endless purges and political upheavals of the Union of Soviet Socialist Republics.

Online Resources

Other books about World War II by Charles River Editors

Other books about the Battle of Kiev on Amazon

Bibliography

Anders, Wladyslaw. *An Army in Exile: The Story of the Second Polish Corps.* London, 1949.

Cienciala, Anna M., Natalia S. Lebedeva, and Wojciech Materski. *Katyn: A Crime without Punishment.* New Haven, 2007.

Ellis, Frank. *Barbarossa 1941: Reframing Hitler's Invasion of Stalin's Soviet Empire.* Lawrence, 2015.

FitzGibbon, Louis. *Katyn.* New York, 1971.

Madden, Ray J. (Chairman). *The Katyn Forest Massacre: Hearings Before the Select Committee to Conduct an Investigation of the Facts, Evidence, and Circumstances of the Katyn Forest Massacre. Eighty-Second Congress.* Washington, 1952.

Maresch, Eugenia. *Katyn 1940: The Documentary Evidence of the West's Betrayal.* Stroud, 2010.

Parrish, Michael. *The Lesser Terror: Soviet State Security, 1939-1953.* Westport, 1996.

Pitt, Barrie. "The Crime at Katyn Wood." *The History of the Second World War, Part 45.* Hicksville, 1972.

Rees, Laurence. *World War II Behind Closed Doors: Stalin, the Nazis, and the West.* New York, 2010.

Remnick, David. *Lenin's Tomb: The Last Days of the Soviet Empire.* New York, 1994.

Tumarkin, Nina. *The Living and the Dead: The Rise and Fall of the Cult of World War II in Russia.* New York, 1994.

Volkogonov, Dmitri. *Autopsy for an Empire: The Seven Leaders Who Built the Soviet Regime.* New York, 1998.

Zawodny, J.K. *Death in the Forest: The Story of the Katyn Forest Massacre.* Notre Dame, 1962.

Free Books by Charles River Editors

We have brand new titles available for free most days of the week. To see which of our titles are currently free, click on this link.

Discounted Books by Charles River Editors

We have titles at a discount price of just 99 cents everyday. To see which of our titles are currently 99 cents, click on this link.

Printed in Great Britain
by Amazon

46407889R00043